# NARADA
# EASY PIANO
## SAMPLER

HAL•LEONARD™
CORPORATION
7777 W. BLUEMOUND RD. P.O. BOX 13819 MILWAUKEE, WI 53213

# TABLE OF CONTENTS

Design by Denyse Gattorna, Connie Gage, Eric Lindert and Wesley Van Linda

© 1994 Nara Music, Inc. and Amida Music, Inc., 4650 N. Port Washington Road, Milwaukee, WI 53212 USA
Tel. 414-961-8350

**ISBN 0-7935-2873-9**
NP-90008SB

# ABOUT THE ARTISTS

## DAVID LANZ

Lanz's best-selling album CRISTOFORI'S DREAM is dedicated to the piano's overlooked Italian inventor, 16th century harpsichord builder Bartolommeo Cristofori. The recording was *Billboard's* No. 1 adult alternative/new age album for more than six months. Lanz calls the piano "the most divinely inspired instrument on the planet."

Selections:
*Behind the Waterfall/Desert Rain Medley* from the album RETURN TO THE HEART
*Cristofori's Dream* from the album CRISTOFORI'S DREAM
*Leaves on the Seine* from the album NIGHTFALL
*Return to the Heart* from the album RETURN TO THE HEART

## MICHAEL JONES

A successful educator/consultant by day, Jones often shared his gently impressionistic music privately with friends in after-dinner recitals, never imagining it would appeal to a large audience. To his pleasant surprise, Jones has released 10 albums and has been nominated for a Juno Award, the Canadian version of the Grammy.

Selections:
*Aspen Summer* from the album PIANO SOLOS
*Butterflies in Space* from the album SUNSCAPES
*Pianoscapes* from the album PIANOSCAPES
*Sunshine Canyon* from the album AMBER

# WAYNE GRATZ

Gratz was introduced to the piano by his kindergarten teacher in Reading, Pennsylvania, Mrs. Biedler. "I loved watching the way she could make the keys bounce when she played," he remembers. "Mrs. Biedler really got into playing." Over the years, Gratz has cultivated one of contemporary music's most graceful and melodic voices at the keyboard.

Selection:
*Ocala* from the album
THE NARADA WILDERNESS COLLECTION

# KOSTIA

The son of a popular Russian film personality, Kostia was born and raised in St. Petersburg (formerly Leningrad). He devoted his life to the piano at the age of 4 and eventually studied at the famed Leningrad Conservatory under two great masters of Russian Romanticism. He has lived in the United States since 1989.

Selection:
*Girl from Barcelona* from the album PIANO SOLOS

# NANCY RUMBEL

Best known as a wind-instrument player (oboe, English horn and ocarinas), Rumbel's attraction to music began with the piano. She encourages piano students to improvise in addition to working with songbooks. "The goal," she says, "is to become not only a musician, but a creator as well. A passion for learning and creating is perhaps the most important ingredient any student can acquire."

Selection:
*The Memory* from the album PIANO SOLOS

Wayne Gratz photograph by Andy Allen; Kostia photograph by Dick Zimmerman Studios/Dick Zimmerman; Nancy Rumbel photograph by Rosanne Olson

# BEHIND THE WATERFALL/ DESERT RAIN MEDLEY

By DAVID LANZ

**Brightly**

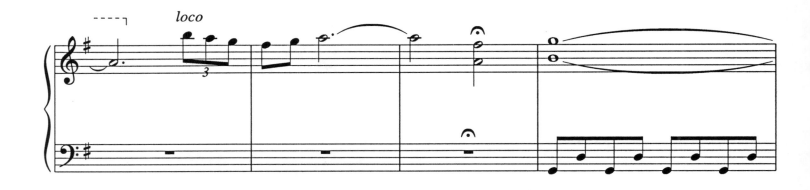

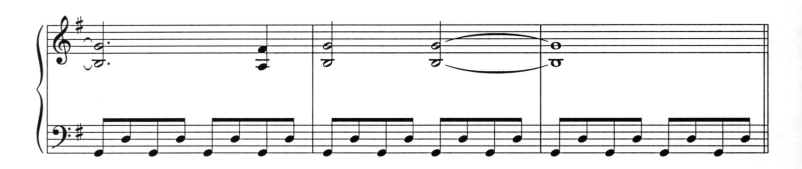

7

**CODA**

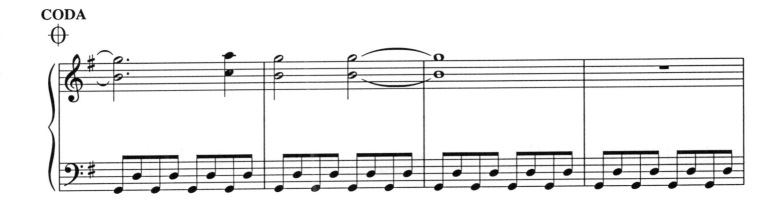

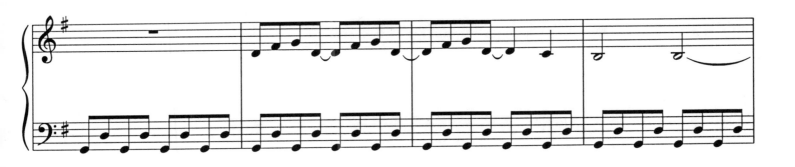

*Ped. - let ring to end*

*8va*- - - - - - - - - - - - - - - - - - - - - - - - - - - - - - - - - - - - - - - - - - - - - - - - - - - - - - -

*loco*

# CRISTOFORI'S DREAM

By DAVID LANZ

14

*L.H. loco on repeat*

# Leaves on the Seine

By DAVID LANZ

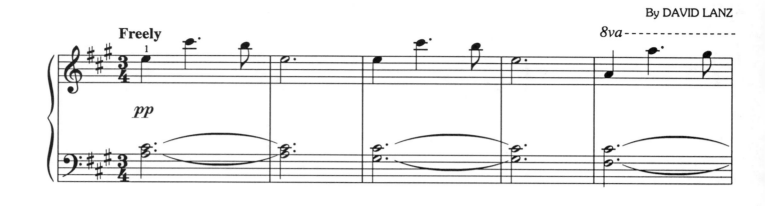

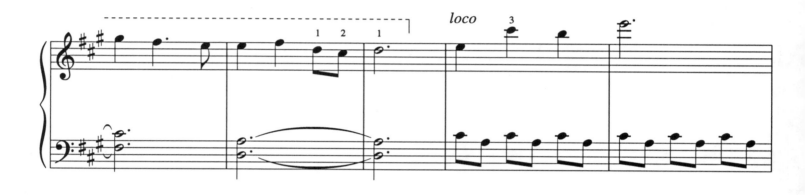

cresc.

f dim.

mp

𝄋 **A tempo**

f

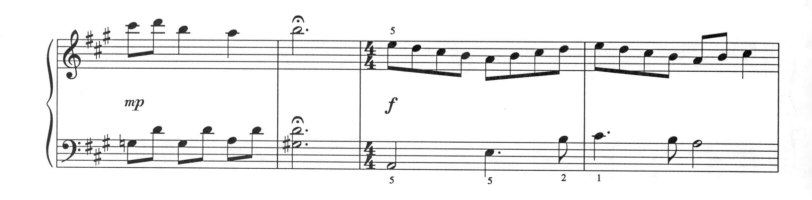

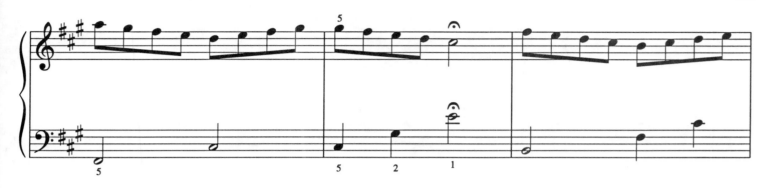

To Coda ⊕           D.S. al Coda

CODA ⊕

Slower

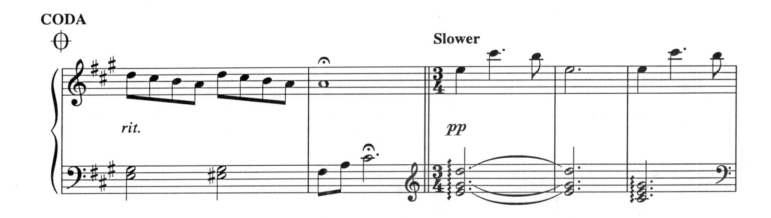

# RETURN TO THE HEART

By DAVID LANZ

**Gently**

# Aspen Summer

By MICHAEL JONES

**Moderately fast**

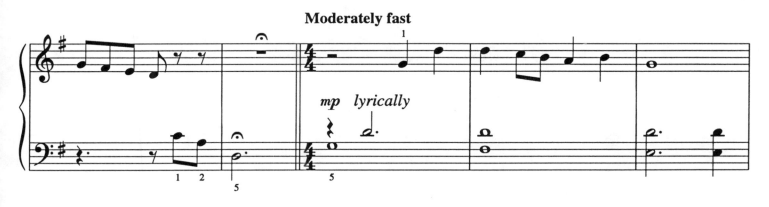

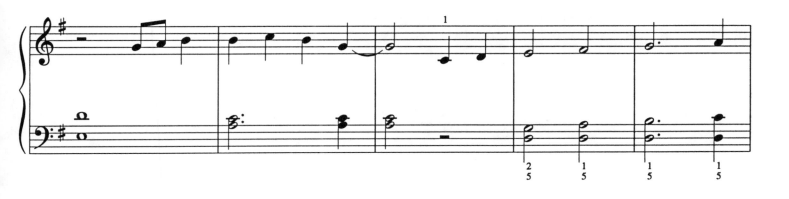

**To Coda** ⊕

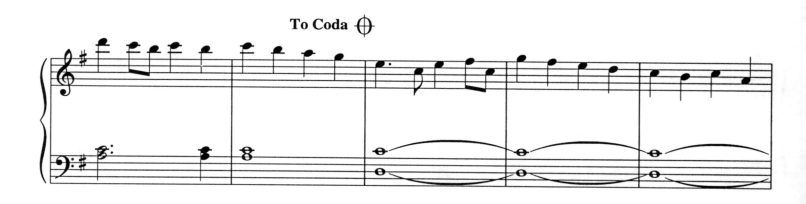

*rit.*                    *a tempo*

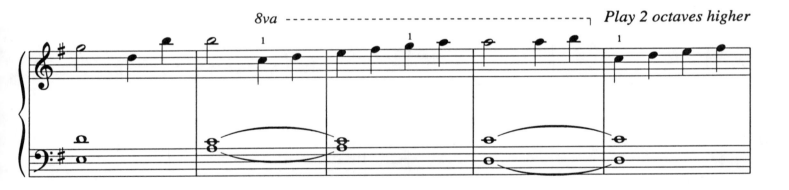

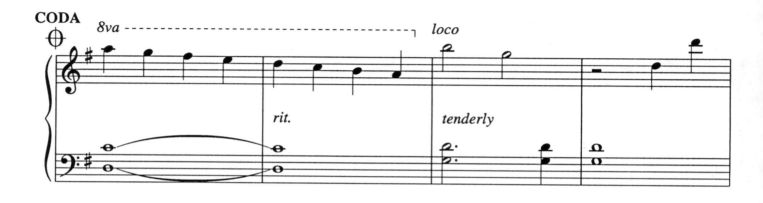

# BUTTERFLIES IN SPACE

By MICHAEL JONES

**With a gentle rhythm**

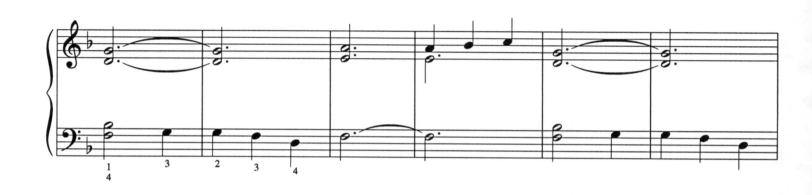

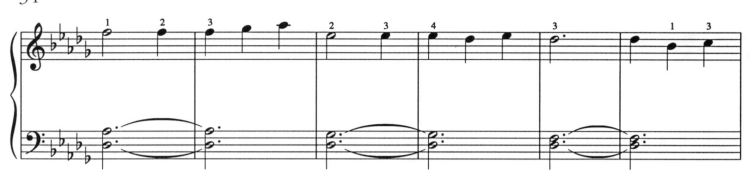

To Coda ⊕

**Light and playful**

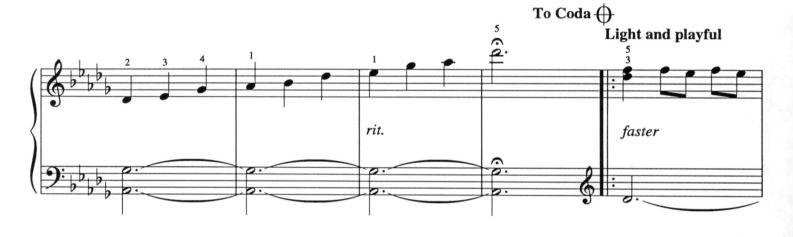

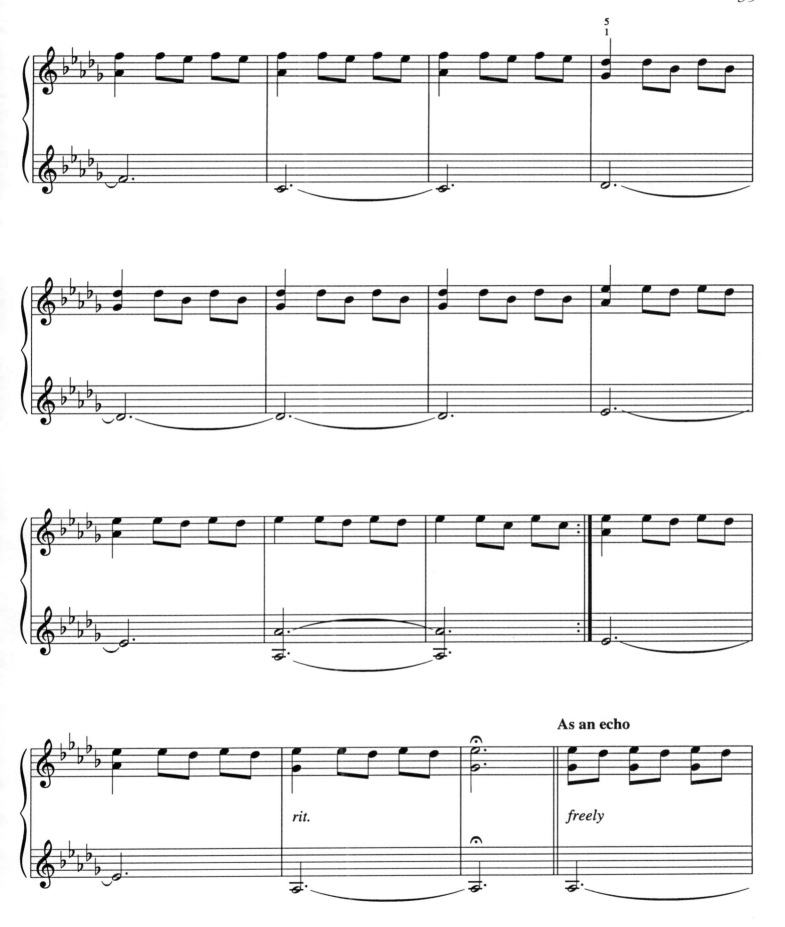

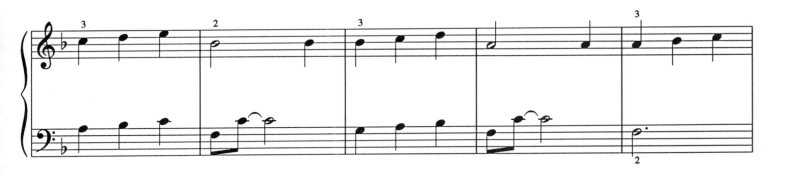

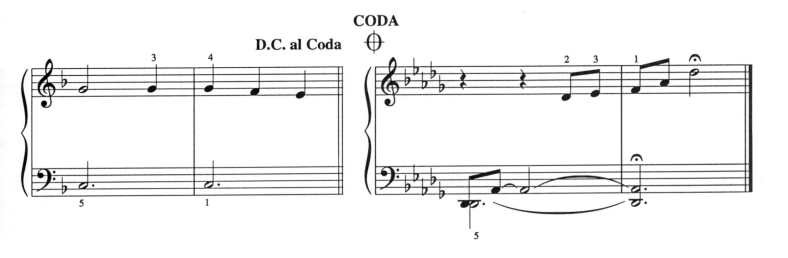

# Pianoscapes

By MICHAEL JONES

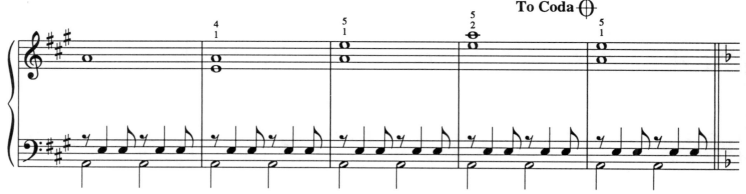

**Full and expressive**

*With pedal*

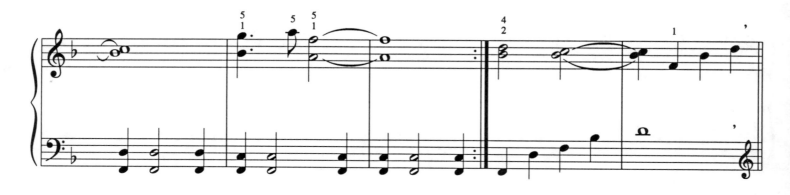

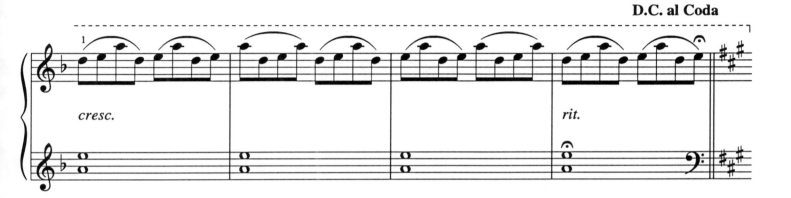

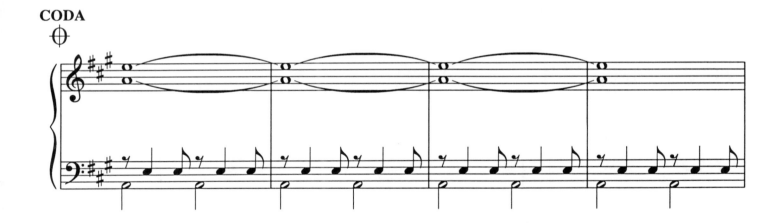

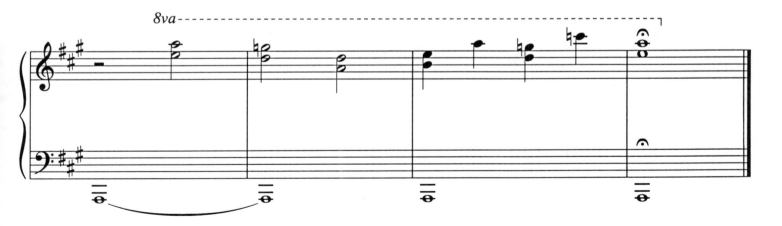

# Sunshine Canyon

By MICHAEL JONES and
DAVID DARLING

**Pensively**

*(play melody 8va)*

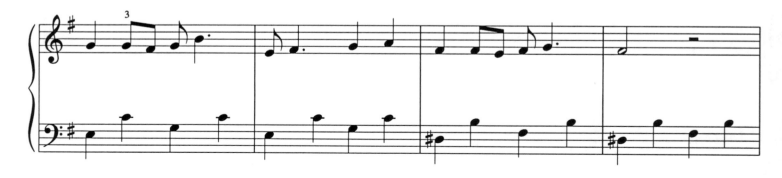

To Coda ⊕

*(play melody as written)*

2nd time D.S. al Coda

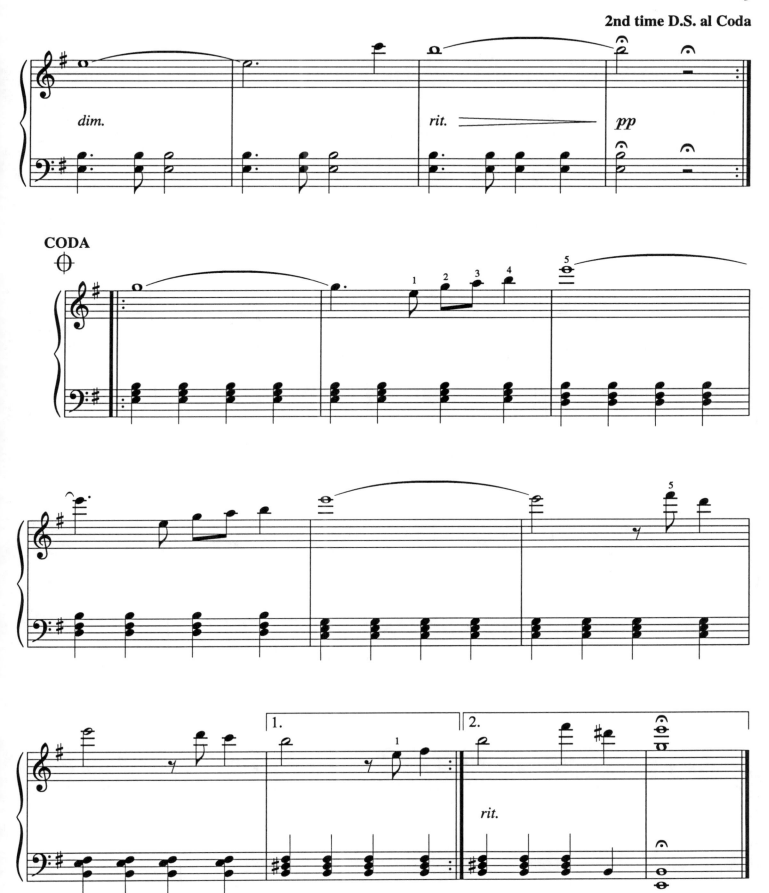

# OCALA

By WAYNE GRATZ

**Brightly**

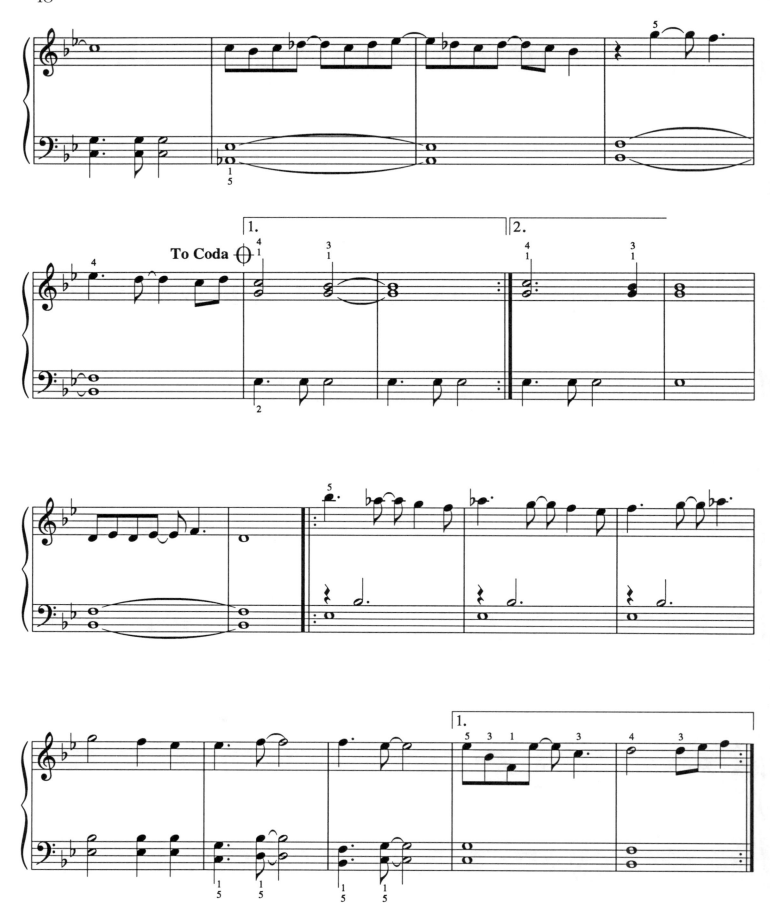

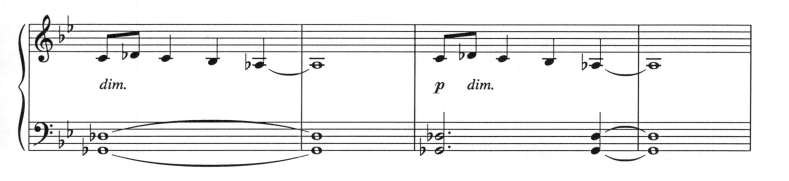

**CODA**

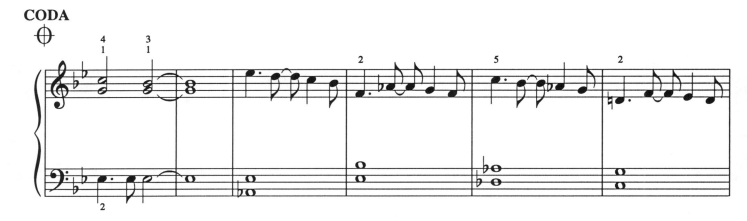

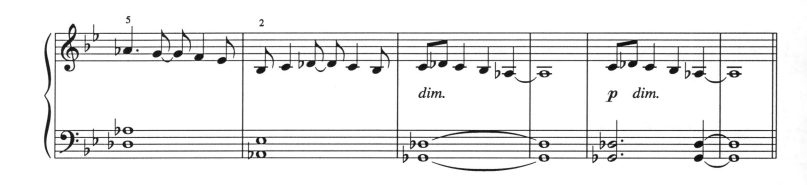

**Repeat and fade**

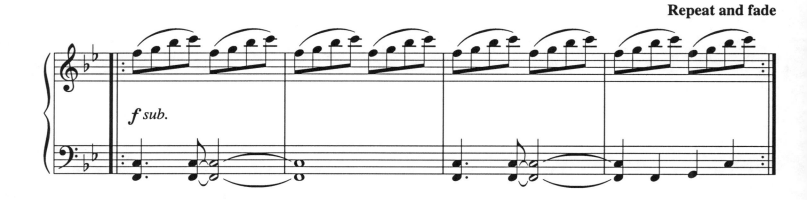

# GIRL FROM BARCELONA

By KOSTIA

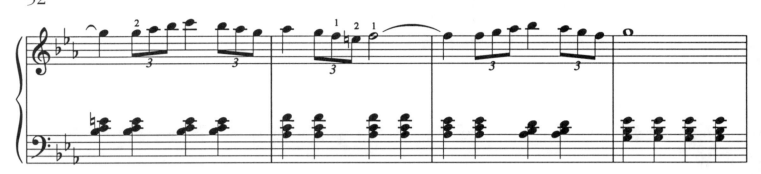

**To Coda** ⊕

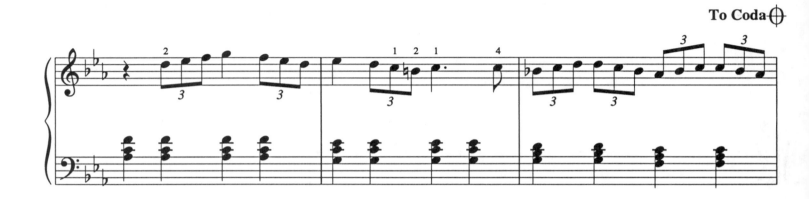

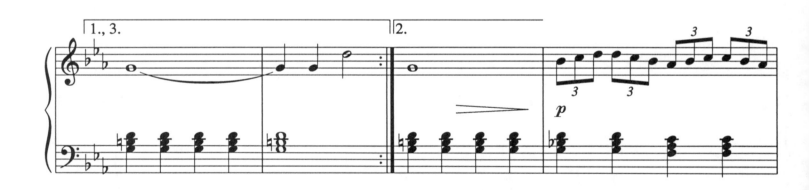

**Faster, flamenco style**

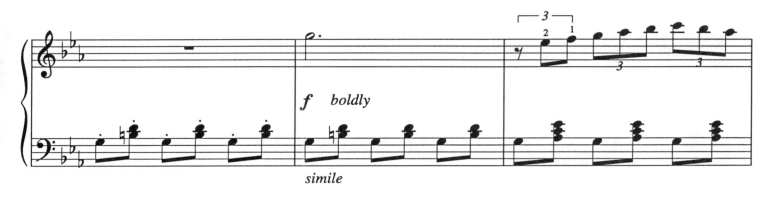

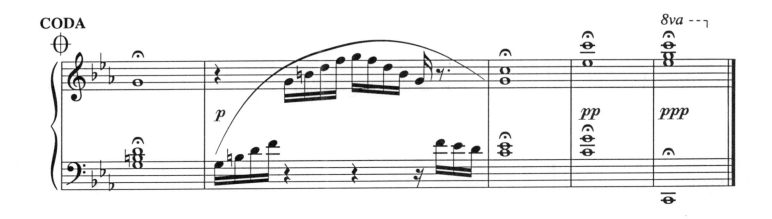

# THE MEMORY

By NANCY RUMBEL

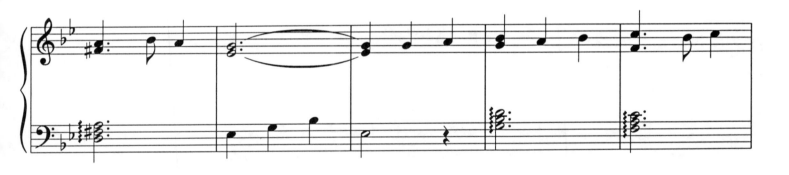

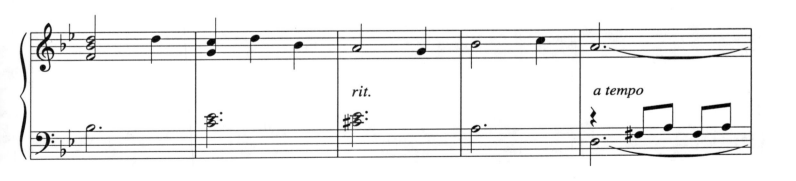

# A CATALOG OF
# NARADA RECORDINGS

## NARADA LOTUS
### New Acoustic Music

N-61001 PIANOSCAPES  Michael Jones
N-61002 SEASONS  Gabriel Lee
N-61003 HEARTSOUNDS  David Lanz
N-61004 SEASCAPES  Michael Jones
N-61005 IMPRESSIONS  Gabriel Lee
N-61006 NIGHTFALL  David Lanz
N-61007 LOTUS SAMPLER #1  Narada Artists
N-61008 SOLSTICE  Michael Jones, David Lanz
N-61009 SUNSCAPES  Michael Jones
N-61010 OPENINGS  William Ellwood
N-61011 EMERALD  Tingstad, Rumbel and Brewer
N-61012 QUIET FIRE  Ancient Future
N-61013 LOTUS SAMPLER #2  Narada Artists
N-61014 AMBER  Michael Jones and David Darling
N-61015 RENAISSANCE  William Ellwood
N-61016 WOODLANDS  Tingstad, Rumbel and Lanz
N-61017 PORTRAITS  Spencer Brewer
N-61018 LOTUS SAMPLER #3  Narada Artists
N-61019 DEPARTURES  John Doan
N-61020 AFTER THE RAIN  Michael Jones
N-61021 CRISTOFORI'S DREAM  David Lanz
N-61022 LEGENDS  Eric Tingstad and Nancy Rumbel
N-61023 REMINISCENCE  Wayne Gratz
N-61024 VISTA  William Ellwood
N-61025 LOTUS SAMPLER #4  Narada Artists
N-61026 HOMELAND  Eric Tingstad and Nancy Rumbel
N-61027 MAGICAL CHILD  Michael Jones
N-61028 PANORAMA  Wayne Gratz
N-61029 WISDOM OF THE WOOD  Narada Artists
N-61030 MORNING IN MEDONTE  Michael Jones
N-61031 PIANO SOLOS  Narada Artists
N-61032 GUITAR WORKS  Narada Artists
N-61033 CAROUSEL  Ira Stein
N-61034 FOLLOW ME HOME  Wayne Gratz
N-61035 ROMANTIC INTERLUDES  Spencer Brewer
N-61036 GIVE AND TAKE  Eric Tingstad and Nancy Rumbel
N-61037 WIND AND REED  Narada Artists
N-61038 TOUCHSTONE  William Ellwood
N-61039 SIMON  Simon Wynberg

## NARADA MYSTIQUE
### New Electronic Music

N-62001 VALLEY IN THE CLOUDS  David Arkenstone
N-62002 THE WAITING  Peter Buffett
N-62003 HIDDEN PATHWAYS  Bruce Mitchell
N-62004 ONE BY ONE  Peter Buffett
N-62005 A VIEW FROM THE BRIDGE  Carol Nethen
N-62006 INTRUDING ON A SILENCE  Colin Chin
N-62007 DANCING ON THE EDGE  Bruce Mitchell
N-62008 CITIZEN OF TIME  David Arkenstone
N-62009 MYSTIQUE SAMPLER ONE  Narada Artists
N-62010 WARM SOUND IN A GRAY FIELD  Peter Maunu
N-62011 THE MESSENGER  Jim Jacobsen
N-62012 LOST FRONTIER  Peter Buffett
N-62013 YONNONDIO  Peter Buffett

## NARADA EQUINOX
### Crossover/Jazz/World

N-63001  NATURAL STATES  David Lanz and Paul Speer
N-63002  INDIAN SUMMER  Friedemann
N-63003  DESERT VISION  David Lanz and Paul Speer
N-63004  EQUINOX SAMPLER ONE  Narada Artists
N-63005  ISLAND  David Arkenstone with Andrew White
N-63006  CIRCLE  Ralf Illenberger
N-63007  CROSS CURRENTS  Richard Souther
N-63008  DORIAN'S LEGACY  Spencer Brewer
N-63009  HEART & BEAT  Ralf Illenberger
N-63010  MIL AMORES  Doug Cameron
N-63011  MOON RUN  Trapezoid
N-63012  CAFÉ DU SOLEIL  Brian Mann
N-63013  WHITE LIGHT  Martin Kolbe
N-63014  NEW LAND  Bernardo Rubaja
N-63015  TWELVE TRIBES  Richard Souther
N-63016  EQUINOX SAMPLER TWO  Narada Artists
N-63017  AQUAMARINE  Friedemann
N-63018  THE PIPER'S RHYTHM  Spencer Brewer
N-63019  PLACES IN TIME  Michael Gettel
N-63020  JOURNEY TO YOU  Doug Cameron
N-63021  SOLEIL  Ralf Illenberger
N-63022  RHYTHM HARVEST  The Michael Pluznick Group
N-63023  ASIAN FUSION  Ancient Future
N-63024  BRIDGE OF DREAMS  David Lanz and Paul Speer
N-63025  SKYWATCHING  Michael Gettel
N-63026  POINTS OF VIEW  Nando Lauria

## NARADA COLLECTION SERIES

N-39100  THE NARADA COLLECTION  Narada Artists
N-39117  THE NARADA COLLECTION TWO  Narada Artists
N-63902  THE NARADA CHRISTMAS COLLECTION  Narada Artists
N-63904  THE NARADA NUTCRACKER  Narada Artists
N-63905  THE NARADA WILDERNESS COLLECTION  Narada Artists
N-63906  THE NARADA COLLECTION THREE  Narada Artists
N-63907  A CHILDHOOD REMEMBERED  Narada Artists
N-63908  ALMA DEL SUR  Various Artists
N-63909  NARADA CHRISTMAS COLLECTION VOLUME 2  Narada Artists
N-63910  NARADA COLLECTION 4  Narada Artists
N-63911  NARADA DECADE  Narada Artists
N-63912  CELTIC ODYSSEY  Various Artists
N-63913  EARTH SONGS  Narada Artists

## NARADA ARTIST SERIES

N-64001  SKYLINE FIREDANCE  David Lanz
N-64002  MICHAEL'S MUSIC  Michael Jones
N-64003  IN THE WAKE OF THE WIND  David Arkenstone
N-64004  IN THE GARDEN  Eric Tingstad and Nancy Rumbel
N-64005  RETURN TO THE HEART  David Lanz
N-64006  THE SPIRIT OF OLYMPIA  David Arkenstone, Kostia, David Lanz
N-64007  CHRONICLES  David Arkenstone

## NARADA CINEMA

N-66001  MILLENNIUM: TRIBAL WISDOM AND THE MODERN WORLD
         Hans Zimmer
N-66002  COLUMBUS AND THE AGE OF DISCOVERY  Sheldon Mirowitz
N-66003  SPACE AGE  Jay Chattaway
N-66004  THE DINOSAURS!  Peter Melnick
N-66005  SEAPOWER: A GLOBAL JOURNEY  Michael Whalen
N-66006  GREAT AFRICAN MOMENTS  Michael Whalen
N-66007  PHANTOM OF THE FOREST  Michael Whalen

Narada appreciates the support of its listeners, and we welcome your comments about the music of our artists.
Narada publishes a free, semi-annual newsletter that features personal interviews with Narada artists
as well as information on new recordings.  You may receive future copies by writing to us and joining our growing,
worldwide family of quality-minded listeners.

Please write to:
Friends of Narada, 4650 N. Port Washington Rd. Milwaukee, WI 53212 USA, or
Friends of Narada, P.O. Box 2301, 1200 CH Hilversum, Netherlands.